Foods of Canada

Barbara Sheen

KIDHAVEN PRESS
A part of Gale, Cengage Learning

GALE
CENGAGE Learning·

Detroit • New York • San Francisco • New Haven, Conn • Waterville, Maine • London

© 2012 Gale, Cengage Learning

LIBRARY OF CONGRESS CATALOGING-IN-PUBLICATION DATA

Sheen, Barbara.
  Foods of Canada / by Barbara Sheen.
    p. cm. -- (A taste of culture)
  Includes bibliographical references and index.
  ISBN 978-0-7377-5947-1 (hardcover)
  1. Cooking, Canadian--Juvenile literature. 2. Food--Canada--Juvenile literature. 3. Food habits--Canada--Juvenile literature. 4. Canada--Social life and customs--Juvenile literature. I. Title.
  TX715.6.S54 2012
  641.5971--dc23

                                                                    2011033477

Kidhaven Press
27500 Drake Rd.
Farmington Hills MI 48331

ISBN-13: 978-0-7377-5947-1
ISBN-10: 0-7377-5947-X

Printed in the United States of America
2 3 4 5 6 7 15 14 13 12 11

Contents

Land of Plenty

Canada is located in North America. It is bordered by the United States in the south, the Atlantic Ocean in the east, the Pacific Ocean in the west, and the Arctic Ocean in the north. It is the second-largest country in the world. Within its vast area are lakes, rivers, forests, mountains, prairies, farmland, arctic tundra, beaches, and islands. Canadians are blessed with an abundant food supply. Among their favorites are fish and seafood, meat, wheat, and maple syrup.

The Lure of Fish and Seafood

Canada's inland and coastal waters are full of life. Halibut, cod, trout, flounder, shrimp, oysters, clams,

FOOD REGIONS OF CANADA

Legend:
- Blueberries
- Cattle
- Corn
- Crab
- Dairy
- Fish
- Grapes
- Lobster
- Mussels
- Pork
- Potatoes
- Poultry
- Salmon
- Scallops
- Soybeans
- Vegetables
- Wheat

GREENLAND

Greenland Sea

ARCTIC OCEAN

Beaufort Sea

Bering Strait

Alaska
U.S.A.

Patrick Island

Banks Island

Melville Island

Prince of Wales Island

Victoria Island

Devon Island

Axel Heiberg Island

Ellesmere Island

Baffin Island

Baffin Bay

Hudson Strait

Ungava Bay

Hudson Bay

Labrador Sea

Newfoundland

Gulf of St. Lawrence

ATLANTIC OCEAN

CANADA

Whitehorse

Juneau

Queen Charlotte Islands

Vancouver Island

Victoria

Yellowknife

Edmonton

Regina

Winnipeg

Olympia

Salem

Helena

Boise

Bismarck

St. Paul

Carson City

U.S.A.

Ottawa

Toronto

Quebec

Fredericton

Charlottetown

Nova Scotia

Halifax

Boston

Salmon was very important to native people in Canada. It not only provided food, but was also a valuable trading product.

lobsters, and salmon make their home there. Fishing has been an important part of Canada's history and culture for at least 10,000 years. Salmon, in particular, was so important to the **First Nations,** or native people of Canada's Pacific coast, that they were called the Salmon People. Salmon not only provided them with food, it was a valuable trading product and an essential part of their culture. First Nations artist Andy Everson explains, "People often ask me why I keep including salmon in my artwork. The answer to this lies with the importance of salmon to me, my relatives and my ancestors."[1]

Canada's rich Atlantic waters drew Europeans to Canada. In 1497, when the explorer John Cabot (also known as Giovanni Caboto) reached the **Grand Banks,**

All About Canada

Canada is a democracy and an independent nation. English and French are the official languages. Its currency is the Canadian dollar. Ottawa, Ontario, is the capital and Toronto, Ontario, is the largest city. Other major cities include Edmonton, Alberta; Vancouver, British Columbia; Montreal, Quebec; Quebec City, Quebec; and Calgary, Alberta. Despite being a vast country, Canada is sparsely populated, with an average of just three people per square kilometer (0.62 square miles). It has only one-half of 1 percent of the world's population.

Canada has a cold climate. Snow covers much of the country for six months out of the year. Ice hockey is the most popular sport, and many Canadian children learn to ice skate when they are toddlers. Skiing, snowmobiling, and snowboarding are also popular.

Canada is a well-off nation. Canadians have a high quality of living.

Children playing ice hockey in Winnipeg, Canada.

a rich fishing area around the Canadian **province** of Newfoundland, he was astounded by the large amount of ocean life. "The sea," he reported to the King of England, "was covered with fish which could be caught not merely by nets, but with weighted baskets lowered into the water."[2] His report drew European fishermen to the Grand Banks. European fur traders and settlers followed.

Today commercial fishing is one of Canada's largest industries, and fish and seafood are staple ingredients in Canadian cooking. Canadian cooks bake, grill, fry, steam, and smoke fish and seafood. They add them to soups, stews, casseroles, and pies.

All Kinds of Meat

Meat also plays an important part in Canadian history and culture. Rolling prairies, which were once the home of about 30 million **bison**, cover much of western Canada. The First Nations of the prairies depended on the bison for food, clothing, and shelter. The meat was eaten fresh and it was turned into **pemmican**, a kind of jerky made by pounding sun-dried bison meat with berries and animal fat. Pemmican could be kept for about a year without spoiling. First Nation hunters and European fur traders carried it with them on their journeys.

Once railroads were built across Canada, homesteaders arrived on the prairies. The bison were killed to make room for ranches where cattle, sheep, and hogs are raised. Today, Canada's livestock and meat-

The result of grinding berries, venison, seeds, and animal fat into small cakes, pemmican could be stored for close to a year.

processing industry is one of the largest in the world. And, the meat these ranches produce is a vital part of the Canadian diet. Canadians eat about 51 pounds (23 kg) of red meat per person annually. Bison, too, is making a comeback. The animals are being raised on ranches. The meat, which is lean and nutritious, is sold throughout the world.

Wild game such as deer, elk, moose, caribou, and rabbit are also very popular. Hunting has been part of Canadian life for centuries and remains a popular sport. The animals are used to make sausages, roasts, pies, casseroles, stews, and soups. According to author

The Fur Trade

French and English fur traders arrived in Canada in the 17th century. They formed companies that traded with First Nations hunters for beaver and other furs. The Hudson's Bay Company and the North West Company were the most famous. The Hudson's Bay Company built forts around Hudson Bay in northeastern Canada. First Nations' hunters from northeastern Canada came to the forts to trade.

The North West Company built trading posts throughout the rest of Canada. The company developed and maintained a supply route that stretched from eastern Canada to the Pacific Ocean. They used the supply route to carry pelts and supplies to and from the trading posts.

Over time villages arose along this route, around the trading posts, and around the forts. Both companies were important in settling Canada.

Anita Stewart, "Wild game is a staple. Freezers are filled in the autumn for use all year round."[3]

Wheat

The prairies are also a good place to grow wheat. In fact, Canada is the world's sixth-largest wheat producer. Flour was very important to Canadian homesteaders who made bread from it. Baking was the job of the women. They baked bread for their own families and their unmarried neighbors. One type of bread, **bannock,** was very popular. It is a flat, round type of fried bread. The bread was an essential food of gold miners who flocked to Canada's Yukon Territory in the late

An elderly Cree woman prepares to eat bannock, a popular fried flatbread.

19th century. The miners mixed the dough for bannock in flour sacks and cooked the bread over an open fire.

Canadians still eat bannock. They also turn wheat into a huge variety of tasty breads, rolls, muffins, cakes, pies, cookies, pancakes, cereals, and pastas. Wheat in some form is part of almost every meal.

Sweet Syrup

Canada's national flag is known as the "Maple Leaf." It is a red and white flag with a large red maple leaf in the center. Sugar maple trees, which produce maple syrup, grow in large quantities in the forests of eastern Canada. Maple syrup has played a part in the Canadian people's diet for centuries.

Sugar maple trees store starch in their roots. The starch is used for nourishment in cold weather. In the

Bannock

Bannock can be baked or fried. For sweet bread, raisins and sugar can be added.

Ingredients
2 cups flour
2 teaspoons baking powder
¾ cup water
¼ cup butter or margarine
Pinch of salt

Directions
1. Preheat the oven to 400°F.
2. Mix together the dry ingredients. Cut in the butter. Mix in the water.
3. Knead the dough for about one minute. Then form it into a round patty, about ½ to 1 inch thick and about 10 inches across.
4. Spray a cookie sheet with nonstick cooking spray. Put the patty on the cookie sheet. Bake about 30 minutes or until a fork inserted in the middle comes out dry.

Serve with butter or jam. Serves 4.

Canadian fry bread, or bannock.

spring the starch changes to sugar, rises, and mixes with tree sap. The people of the First Nations were the first to make maple syrup, which they called "sweet water." To do so, first, they made a cut in the tree's bark. Next, they inserted a reed through which the sap flowed. The sap was collected into buckets and boiled until it thickened into maple syrup. The European settlers followed suit. Both the people of the First Nations and the European settlers used the syrup to sweeten and flavor their food. Many modern Canadians do so, too.

Today, Canada produces 85 percent of the world's maple syrup. Many people consider it to be the best of any nation. Unlike some types of maple syrup sold in the United States that contain corn syrup and other additives, Canadian maple syrup is pure. It is thick, dark, and strong tasting. It takes 40 gallons (151L) of sap to make 1 gallon (3.7L) of pure maple syrup. An because it takes so much sap to make so little syrup, maple syrup is expensive.

Visiting **sugar shacks**, makeshift buildings where sap is boiled in large vats, is a yearly event in northeastern Canada. At the end of the season there are sugaring-off parties in which dishes made with maple syrup are served. Long tables are covered with platters of maple syrup–glazed ham and sausage, maple syrup pies, tarts, puddings, and cakes, pancakes topped with maple syrup, beans baked in maple syrup, and maple syrup candies. Maple taffy, or snow taffy, is a hot syrup dropped on clean snow and left to harden. It is a favorite among children. Canadian chef Ryan Skelton recalls:

Maple syrup harvesters boiling sap in Northern Ontario.

I can remember class and family trips to Black Creek Pioneer Village [a farm where maple syrup is made]. The smells in the sugar shack were a combination of the maple syrup boiling down and the smoke from the fire. Outside the shack there was a huge cast iron kettle suspended over an open fire with steam rising from the maple syrup in its final stages bubbling away, perfect for making maple taffy on packed melting snow. It was overly sweet and occasionally made my teeth hurt, but I couldn't resist.[4]

Maple Syrup Sundae

Here is a simple dessert that features maple syrup. It would be delicious with coffee ice cream. Peanuts can be used instead of walnuts to add a salty taste. Whipped cream and fresh blueberries can be added.

Ingredients
4 scoops vanilla ice cream
4 tablespoons maple syrup
4 teaspoons chopped walnuts

Directions
1. Get four parfait glasses. Put a scoop of ice cream in each.
2. Spoon the maple syrup over the ice cream and top with 1 teaspoon of nuts per serving.

Serves 4.

There are so many delicious delicacies that tempt Canadians. A huge variety of plants, animals, and sea creatures flourish in this vast land. Canadian cooks take advantage of this bounty. Maple syrup, meat, wild game, fish, seafood, and wheat are among their favorite ingredients. These foods are not only important to Canadian cooking, they hold a key place in Canadian history and culture.

Chapter 2

A Diverse Nation

People from many cultures live in Canada. Historians think Canada's first people came across a land bridge from Asia to North America thousands of years ago. They represent many tribal groups and became known, collectively, as the First Nations. In later years parts of Canada were colonized by both England and France. Over time people from other parts of the world settled in Canada, too. In order to survive in a new land, the newcomers changed the recipes that they brought from their homelands to suit their new environment. They used native foods and cooking methods that they learned from the First Nations people. Favorite dishes such as chowders, traditionally cooked seafood, pancakes, and baked beans reflect the influences of the First Nations, the various groups that settled in Canada, and the regions they settled in.

Thick, Hearty Soups

Canadians enjoy a variety of chowders, which are thick and hearty soups made with milk, potatoes, bacon, crumbled biscuits or crackers, and often fish or other seafood. It is likely that chowders originated in France and were adapted by Canadian settlers. Corn chowder is an example of a dish Canadian cooks made by combining a recipe from their homeland with food available locally. Corn, which is native to the Americas, was new to Canada's earliest settlers. Homesteaders were given hard bread, canned milk, flour, and salt pork, which is pork preserved in salt similar to bacon, when they settled their land. By combining these ingredients with corn, they created a new type of chowder. Over time cooks added potatoes, onions, herbs, and butter to the soup. The end result is rich and filling with a sweet, smoky flavor.

Fish chowders are other favorites. To make fish chowder, fish is cooked in water with milk, herbs, onions, butter, and potatoes. It is quite similar to bouillabaisse (boo-ya-BAZE), a French seafood stew. Fish chowder can contain a mixture of fish and seafood, or just one fish or shellfish. Lobster chowder is especially popular on Canada's Atlantic coast, where lobsters are abundant. No matter the main ingredients, all Canadian fish chowders are thick, creamy, and nourishing.

Corn Chowder

Here's a hearty chowder perfect for a cold day. Vegetarians can eliminate the bacon.

Ingredients
1 cup whole kernel corn frozen, or canned (drained)
1 can (14 oz.) cream-style corn
1 can (10 oz.) cream of potato soup
4 cups milk
4 slices of bacon
½ onion chopped
1 ½ cups of potato, peeled and cut into small chunks
1 teaspoon pepper

Directions
1. Fry the onions and bacon until the bacon is crisp and the onions are translucent.
2. Combine all the ingredients in a large pot. Cook over medium heat until the soup boils. Reduce heat to low. Cover the pot. Cook until the potatoes are soft, or about 30 minutes.

Serves 4.

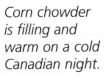

Corn chowder is filling and warm on a cold Canadian night.

Fish chowder, says chef Ryan Skelton, "will warm you right through on a cold day…. I absolutely love a great bowl of seafood chowder."[5]

Traditionally Cooked Seafood

Long before settlers from other nations arrived in Canada, members of the First Nations living on the Atlantic and Pacific coasts of Canada had their own way of preparing fish and seafood. Some of Canada's favorite dishes today are taken from recipes and cooking methods of the First Nations people.

Cedar plank grilled salmon is one such dish. Canada has many forests where cedar trees grow. The First Nations of the Pacific Northwest grilled salmon over an open fire on a cedar plank. They soaked the wood slab in water before placing it on the fire. As the wet plank heated up, it re-

Seafood, corn, and potatoes are steamed in the traditional clam bake method learned from the First Nations.

Maple-Glazed Salmon

This recipe can be made on a grill or in a broiler. Be sure to use real maple syrup.

Ingredients
4 salmon filets, ¼–⅓ lb each
⅓ cup maple syrup
¼ cup extra virgin olive oil
¼ cup low sodium soy sauce
3 teaspoons fresh lime juice
Pinch each of ginger and garlic powder
1 teaspoon red pepper flakes (optional)

Directions
1. Combine all the ingredients except the salmon in a large bowl. Put the salmon in the bowl. Spoon the sauce over the salmon. Refrigerate for 30 minutes to overnight.
2. Turn broiler on to high. Line a broiler pan with non-stick foil. Put the salmon on the pan. Broil until the salmon flakes easily, about 10 minutes.

Serves 4.

leased moisture and a sweet, smoky aroma and flavor that the fish absorbed.

Modern Canadians often cook salmon this same way on backyard barbecues. Cedar planks are sold in Canadian supermarkets for this purpose. Cooks usually **marinate** the fish in a variety of different mixtures like soy sauce and sugar; or they brush the fish with maple syrup as it cooks. The end result tastes sweet and smoky and its texture is moist and tender.

Steamed seafood is another Canadian favorite, especially when it is part of a **clambake**. A clambake is another traditional cooking method that Canadians learned from the First Nations people. Clambakes are held on beaches where freshly dug clams are cooked in a large pit lined with stones. A fire is lit in the pit. When it dies down, the clams are placed in the pit between layers of seaweed. The wet seaweed produces steam, which cooks the clams. Corn and potatoes are often cooked in the pit, too. On the Atlantic coast of Canada, lobsters are often part of the clambake.

When the shellfish are tender, diners crack the shells open and dig out the delicious soft meat, which smells of the sea. Melted butter and lemon slices are served with the fish. Traditionally, boiled fiddleheads, a type of fern that grows in Canada's forests, are served, too. Fiddleheads taste like asparagus. They are poisonous when eaten raw, but are safe to eat when thoroughly cooked. European settlers learned how to cook the ferns from the First Nations people. The settlers often substituted fiddleheads for vegetables from their homelands.

Pancakes

Pancakes are another favorite food. Pancakes are made in different forms all over the world. Many different types of pancakes have been popular in Canada ever since European settlers arrived there. Blueberry pancakes made with buckwheat, a hearty grain that grows

Pancakes and maple syrup are part of a typical Canadian breakfast.

well in cold places, were prepared in **chuck wagons** for the cowboys on Canada's prairies. Canadian loggers, too, almost always started their day with buckwheat pancakes topped with maple syrup. A Canadian tall tale describes the pancake griddles the loggers used as being so large that it was impossible to see across the pans. Many modern Canadian restaurants offer what is known as a logger's breakfast. It consists of pancakes, ham, sausage, bacon, and three eggs.

Canadian gold miners ate pancakes made of sourdough, too. Sourdough is a kind of bread dough made with harmless bacteria that give it a tart flavor and keep

The Provinces

Canada is divided into ten provinces and three territories. Each province is like a state with its own governor. The territories do not have governors. From west to east, the territories are Yukon, Northwest Territories, and Nunuvat. They are located in the northernmost part of Canada and include Canada's Arctic Islands. From west to east, the provinces are British Columbia, Alberta, Saskatchewan, Manitoba, Ontario, Quebec, Newfoundland, New Brunswick, Nova Scotia, and Prince Edward Island.

Newfoundland, New Brunswick, Nova Scotia, and Prince Edward Island are known collectively as the Maritimes, because they border the Atlantic Ocean and fishing is their main industry. Quebec was once a French colony. French is spoken there. Ontario is where Ottawa, the nation's capital is located. Manitoba, Saskatchewan, and Alberta are located on the prairies. British Columbia borders the Pacific Ocean. It gets lots of rain and has the warmest weather in Canada.

it from spoiling. The miners used the dough to make thick, filling pancakes that were a big part of their diet.

Modern Canadians still eat sourdough and buckwheat pancakes. Pancake breakfasts are popular fundraising events all over Canada. French Canadians on Canada's Atlantic coast eat pancakes known as ployes (ploys) instead of bread. Ployes are made with flour and water but no milk or eggs. They are not flipped over, but rather are cooked on only one side. When the bottom is brown and the top is still moist, the ploye is done. Ployes are slathered with butter, then rolled or folded. They are quite filling but contain fewer calories than bread. French Canadians in the province of Quebec

Foods with Interesting Names

Many Canadian foods have interesting names. Here are a few:

beaver tails: Chunks of long, flat pieces of fried dough sprinkled with cinnamon and sugar.

blueberry buckle: Blueberry-filled cake.

bumbleberry pie: A mixed berry pie.

caesar: A drink made of tomato juice and clam juice.

double-double: An extra-large cup of coffee containing a double helping of cream and sugar.

doughboys: Dumplings that are usually served with chicken.

figgy duff: A sweet steamed pudding.

geoducks, or gooey ducks: Large clams from Canada's Pacific coast.

ginger sparkles: Cookies flavored with ginger and molasses.

jam busters: Jelly doughnuts.

lassie: Molasses.

scrunchins: Fried pork cubes that are sprinkled over fish.

Smarties: Little candies.

(kwih-BECK) prefer paper-thin pancakes known as crepes (crapes). Canadian crepes are similar to those made in France. Crepes may be filled with sugar or any number of other ingredients, including mushrooms, cheese, ham, or asparagus.

Baked Beans

Baked beans are another popular Canadian food. To make them, cooks first boil white beans with salt pork, ham, or bacon. Next, they top the beans with maple syrup or molasses and bake them on low heat for hours until all the flavors mix and the beans are meltingly sweet and tender. Baked beans were eaten by the people of the First Nations, fur traders, homesteaders, cowboys, miners, and loggers. According to author Bunny Barss, "Hungry loggers in Quebec ate beans and salt pork twice a day.... Prospectors claim that

Gold prospectors claimed that baked beans opened up Ontario's mines.

beans opened up Ontario's mines. ...They were a standby for prairie cooks. Beans travelled in the chuck-wagons with the cattle herds, they went ... to the gold fields and up north to the trappers' cabins."[6] Baked beans are still popular all over Canada. Traditionally, they are eaten on Saturday nights with homemade biscuits.

Canadian cooking owes much to the First Nations, and to the many cultural groups that have made Canada their home. "Canada tastes like the heritage of a hundred cultures, come together in one land,"[7] says Canadian food blogger David Katz. Canada's favorite dishes grew out of this delicious and varied mix.

chapter

3

Uniquely Canadian Treats

Canadians enjoy a wide variety of sweet and savory treats. Many of these—like burgers, ice cream, pizza, doughnuts, and brownies—are familiar to Americans. Some of the most popular are uniquely Canadian. All are delicious.

Poutine

Poutine (POOH-tin), which means "mushy mess" in French, is a distinctively Canadian fast food. It was invented in the 1950s in Quebec by the owner of a roadside chip wagon, a food truck that specializes in cooking and selling fried potatoes. The dish, which consists of fried potatoes topped with cheese, gravy, and sometimes additional ingredients, quickly became

Poutine, or "mushy mess", is french fried potatoes covered with cheese curds and gravy.

the Canadian people's favorite savory snack. Poutine is sold in fine restaurants, diners, cafés, fast-food chains, and chip wagons all over Canada.

To make poutine, sliced potatoes are deep fried in lard, or animal fat. When the potatoes are crispy, they are topped with cheddar cheese curds. Cheddar cheese curds may be unfamiliar to non-Canadians but they are very popular in Canada. In fact, they are sold in bags as a snack food in Canadian supermarkets the same way potato chips are sold in the United States. The curds are the solid part of soured milk. They are white and have a rubbery texture and a salty taste. They squeak when they rub against a person's teeth. This is due to air trapped inside the cheese.

The potatoes and cheese are covered by piping-

A Natural Wonderland

Canada is a natural wonderland. It contains more lakes and inland waterways than any other nation in the world. Niagara Falls, one of the world's largest waterfalls, is shared by Canada and the United States.

Forty-five percent of Canada is forest, where wildlife such as black bears, wolves, deer, beavers, rabbits, and moose live. In Canada's far north, there are polar bears and herds of caribou and musk ox. Whales, seals, and sea lions make their home in Canada's northern waters. To protect its wildlife and natural beauty, Canada has 41 national parks and three marine conservation areas.

The aurora borealis, or the Northern Lights, are visible in much of Canada year-round. It is a nightly display of dancing green, white, and red light which is caused by electrical activity in the outermost layer of Earth's atmosphere.

Approximately 90% of Niagara River flows over the Horseshoe Falls section of Niagara Falls. Most of Horseshoe Falls is located in Ontario, Canada.

hot gravy that is very thick. The gravy has a smoky, vinegary flavor and aroma. Sometimes ground beef, bacon, onions, and/or peas are also added, either individually or in combinations. The final result is a perfect blend of different tastes, textures, and smells. It is crisp, moist, cheesy, saucy, and smoky all at the same time. According to A. Knight the creator of the Canadian information website Knight's Canadian Info Collection, "When the curds are placed on the fries and the hot gravy is poured on top, the three flavors combine to produce what can only be described as the BEST junk food taste sensation on earth . . . and something that is totally Canadian!"[8]

Nanaimo Bars

Sweet and chocolatey Nanaimo (nuh-NEYE-moe) bars are another popular snack that is uniquely Canadian. No one knows where the bars originated. Many Canadians say they were invented in the Pacific coastal town of Nanaimo by a housewife who entered a Canadian magazine's dessert-recipe contest in the 1950s. Rather than name her creation after herself, she named it after her hometown. When she won the contest, both the town of Nanaimo and the bars became famous.

Nanaimo bars are simple to make but they take time. They contain three layers. Each layer must be chilled before the next is added. They do not require any baking. They start with a base made of cocoa powder, chopped walnuts, coconut, and cookie crumbs stuck together with melted butter. The base layer is

Layered Nanaimo bars are a traditional dessert in Canada, often served with tea.

chilled until it hardens. Then, a rich, creamy layer of butter cream, which is made of butter, sugar, milk, and custard powder, is spread on top of the base. Custard powder was invented in England, and is a popular ingredient there and in Canada. It is not commonly sold in the United States. It is similar in taste and texture to instant vanilla pudding, which is a good substitute. Finally, when the custard layer has set, a layer of melted dark chocolate is poured over the whole thing. The sweet treat is ready to eat when the chocolate is hard and smooth.

Nanaimo bars are cut into squares and are often served with a cup of tea. Like their former English rulers, many Canadians sip tea throughout the day. The bars are sold in doughnut shops, cafés, bakeries, and supermarkets all over Canada. There are many varieties. Some substitute peanut butter for the custard layer; others add cherries or mint, but the original bars remain the most popular.

The bars taste crunchy, chewy, smooth, creamy, sweet, and bitter. Food writer and blog author Jessie Oleson, who traveled throughout Canada tasting the

Tea Time

Much of Canada was under British rule from the 16th century until the middle of the 19th century. France also claimed parts of Canada, but gave up its claims to the English in 1763. Both these nations had a big influence on Canadian culture.

For example, in the Canadian province of British Columbia, the English custom of taking an afternoon tea break is a tradition. Hotels, restaurants, and elegant tea rooms serve customers hot tea from delicate teapots. The tea is accompanied by fresh muffins and scones, which are biscuit-like pastries that originated in England, served with fresh strawberry jam and thick whipped cream. Another English favorite, tiny tea sandwiches are also served. Tea sandwiches are dainty, bite-sized snacks typically made of white bread cut into quarters and filled with light tidbits such as a cucumber slice, a dab of egg salad, or a bit of cheese.

Cranberry Fudge

Cranberries are plentiful in Canada. Cranberry fudge combines chocolate and cranberries for a sweet, delicious treat.

Ingredients
1 cup dried cranberries
18 ounces semi-sweet chocolate chips
1 14-ounce can sweetened condensed milk
1 cup chopped walnuts

Directions
1. Put the chocolate chips and condensed milk in a saucepan and cook over low heat until the chocolate melts. Stir often.
2. Remove from the heat. Stir in the berries and nuts.
3. Spray an 8-inch square pan with nonstick spray. Pour the chocolate mixture into the pan.
4. Refrigerate until the fudge becomes firm. Cut into small squares.

Makes about 30 squares.

bars, describes them in this way: "The top layer is a solid chocolatey layer, which is firm but not hard. The middle layer is a buttery, frosting-y, creamy, custard-y stuff that is so much the opposite of low-fat that it makes you want to weep with pleasure. The bottom layer is a sturdy, tightly packed layer of chocolate, graham cracker and coconut, bound together with melted butter. That is to say—super yum."[9]

Maple Syrup Pie

Maple syrup pie is another unique Canadian sweet. Also known as sugar pie and backwoods pie, this delicious treat is a traditional French-Canadian specialty that originated in Quebec. Maple syrup pie consists of a pastry crust that is filled with a sweet gooey mixture of maple syrup, eggs, cream, vanilla, and brown sugar. It is baked until the crust is light, flaky, and golden, and the filling is soft, smooth, and dry. The pie can be served hot or cold. It is dark, very sweet, and rich, especially when it is topped with a thick layer of whipped cream or a big scoop of ice cream and a splash of maple syrup. It was chosen by food website Epicurious.com as the dish that best represents Canada. It is also one of Canada's most delicious creations.

Maple syrup pie, also known as sugar pie or backwoods pie.

Lots of Berries

Pastries made with berries are another Canadian specialty. Many different varieties of berries grow wild throughout Canada. They are also grown on large berry farms. Since the First Nations settled in Canada, Canadians have taken advantage of this sweet and juicy bounty. Some, like strawberries, blueberries, cranberries, and blackberries, are well known in the United States, while others, like tart gooseberries, and sweet purple saskatoon berries, are less so. Berry picking is a seasonal activity in Canada. Families have fun together while gathering sweet juicy berries. Canadian food blogger Lynette Stanley-Maddocks recalls, "We ate berries straight off the bush still warm from the sunshine. . . . We'd collect wild blueberries, cranberries, and gooseberries. Mum would make pancakes and put our...blueberries in."[10]

Berries are also featured in dozens of different kinds of pastries. Berry pies served warm and topped with vanilla ice cream are extremely popular. Mock cherry pie is one distinctly Canadian favorite. It does not contain cherries at all, but rather bright-red cranberries, which are especially abundant in Canada. Saskatoon berry pie is a prairie specialty. The berries grow on Canada's prairies and are treasured for their sugary, juicy flavor. Berries are also turned into muffins, cakes, and buckles —single-layered cakes filled with berries and topped with a spicy, sugary crumb crust. Blueberry buckle is a famous Canadian creation, so is blueberry cipate (SEE-

Blueberry Muffins

Blueberry muffins are a popular Canadian treat. For sweeter muffins add more sugar. For less-sweet muffins, use less. Soy milk can be substituted for milk.

Ingredients
1 ½ cups blueberries, cleaned
2 cups flour
1 cup sugar
2 eggs
½ cup butter, softened
1 cup milk
2 teaspoons baking powder

Directions
1. Preheat the oven to 375°F. Spray muffin cups and tops of the pans with a generous amount of nonstick spray.
2. Mix the butter, sugar, eggs, and milk. Mix in the flour and baking powder. Add the blueberries, mix gently.
3. Spoon the mixture into the muffin pans. Do not fill to the top. Bake until the muffins are golden brown and a fork or toothpick inserted into the muffins comes out dry, about 20–30 minutes.
4. Let the muffins cool before removing them from the pan.

Makes about 18 muffins.

Blueberry muffins made with fresh Canadian blueberries.

Canadians enjoy berry picking in the Tombstone Valley area of Yukon, Canada.

paht). It is a French-Canadian three-layered blueberry pie. Berries are also the stars of cobblers, which are berries mixed with sugar and topped with biscuit dough, and crisps, which are like cobblers but are topped with a crumb crust.

Although not all of these pastries are unique to Canada, the abundance of berries in pastries and desserts is very Canadian. "Canada," says Stanley-Maddocks, "tastes like berries warm from the sun."[11]

Canada also tastes like savory poutine, sweet maple syrup pies, and chocolatey Nanaimo bars. When it comes to snacks and desserts, Canadians have lots of choices. They not only eat many of the same foods as people all over the world, but they also enjoy Canadian treats that are both delicious and unique. These treats are part of what makes Canada such a special place.

chapter 4

Festive Food

Canadians like to get together with family and friends on holidays and special occasions. Festive foods associated with the occasion are part of the celebration.

Halloween Fun

Canadians have been celebrating Halloween since settlers from England, Ireland, and Scotland brought the tradition to Canada. Canadians celebrate Halloween on October 31 in much the same way as people in the United States do. Costumed children go trick-or-treating, people decorate their homes and yards, and parties are held. Apples are often included in the celebration.

At least a dozen different varieties of apples grow in Canada. Some, such as red, round, juicy McIntosh

Since Canadian's apple harvesting season coincides with Halloween, caramel apples are a popular holiday treat.

apples, were developed in Canada. Others, like sour green crabapples, are native to the country. Additional varieties were planted by European explorers, settlers, and priests.

Canada's apple harvest coincides with Halloween, making the fruit especially plentiful at that time of year. Caramel apples are a popular holiday favorite. To make them, cooks remove the stems from round red apples and insert a craft stick. The stick makes it easy to hold the apple. Next, they dip the apples in hot caramel sauce, a sweet, sticky syrup made by either melting caramel candies or by heating butter, sugar, and vanilla until the mixtures becomes gooey. The caramel-coated apples are next rolled in nuts. Next, they apples are chilled until the caramel becomes solid. The Halloween treats are sweet, sticky, crunchy, and delicious. It is no wonder they are a favorite of Canadians of all ages.

Canadian Thanksgiving

Canadians celebrate Thanksgiving on the second Monday of October. The holiday has its roots in European and First Nations' harvest festivals, and in American Thanksgiving celebrations. Long before Europeans arrived in Canada, the First Nations celebrated fall harvests with singing, dancing, and large feasts. Harvest festivals were also a tradition in Europe for thousands of years. As early as the 1600s, French settlers in Canada marked their harvests with banquets. Loyalists were American colonists loyal to the King of England, who fled north to Canada during the American Revo-

Canada Day Celebrations

In 1867 representatives from the provinces of Quebec, Ontario, New Brunswick, and Nova Scotia voted to unite under the name of Canada. In later years, other provinces and territories joined the union. Each year on July 1 Canadians mark their country's birthday with Canada Day celebrations. Activities include concerts, fireworks displays, air shows, dances, parades, rodeos, carnivals, and pancake breakfasts. Picnics are a traditional activity. These are held on beaches, in parks, forests, meadows, and along the shores of lakes and rivers. Fresh foods that are at peak season in the summer are almost always on the menu. Foods like grilled salmon or trout, bison burgers, corn on the cob, and a variety of cold salads are typical fare. Homemade ice cream topped with fresh berries, white cakes topped with vanilla frosting and strawberries, or chocolate cakes are popular desserts.

Canada Day firework celebration over Parliament Hill.

lutionary War. They kept up the American tradition of celebrating Thanksgiving in their new home. Modern Canadian Thanksgiving celebrations combine these traditions. They are family gatherings in which special foods, many of which have recently been harvested, are served. A typical menu might include roast turkey, **wild rice**, cranberries, squash, and **butter tarts**.

Butter tarts are pastries filled with sugar, maple syrup, eggs, and butter. Some butter tart fillings contain raisins, fruit, or nuts.

Turkeys are native to North America and have long been a popular food in Canada. Hunting wild turkeys is a seasonal event here. Indeed, the main course on Thanksgiving is as likely to be a recently shot wild turkey as a store-bought one. Cooks often brush maple syrup on the turkey as it roasts. This gives it a sweet, smoky taste and aroma.

Side dishes like squash, cranberries, and wild rice

Yellow Squash with Onions and Mushrooms

Squash is a popular Canadian Thanksgiving side dish. This is an easy and tasty way to fix it.

Ingredients
4 medium yellow squash, washed and cut in rounds
1 small onion, peeled and sliced
1 cup sliced mushrooms
1 teaspoon garlic powder
2 tablespoons olive oil
Salt and pepper to taste

Directions
1. 1.Cover the bottom of a frying pan with oil. Warm the oil over low heat.
2. 2.Add the other ingredients. Cook until the vegetables are tender.

Serves 4.

are also native to Canada. Wild rice is not really rice at all. It is a grain with a delicate nutty flavor produced by a type of wild grass. It grows in water and flourishes in the thousands of lakes in eastern and central Canada. It is harvested from boats, then dried. Author Anita Stewart explains: "Wild rice looks much like wide blades of grass until, in late August and September, the heavy seed heads droop down, making them easily accessible to the airboats that pass back and forth and are used as harvesters. . . . When the wild rice is dried over burners, the air becomes filled with an almost indescribably delicious nutty aroma."[12]

The Thanksgiving feast is not complete until dessert is served. Butter tarts are a top choice. The tarts originated in Canada and were a staple of pioneer cooking. Butter tarts are little pastries filled with a mixture of butter, sugar, eggs, raisins, and maple syrup. Depending on the cook, the pastry that holds the filling can be crisp or tender, and the filling can be firm or so runny that it dribbles down diners' chins when biting into the tart. Canadians love butter tarts and every variation has its fans. "They are part of who we are,"[13] explains Canadian radio host Peter Gzowski.

French-Canadian Meat Pie

Christmas is another festive time in Canada. **Tourtière** (tuhr-tee-AIR) is a thick meat pie wrapped in a flaky crust that is a part of Christmas Eve celebrations in many Canadian homes. It is also eaten on New Year's Eve. Tourtière was brought to Canada by French set-

The Canadian tourtière meat pie is closely associated with Quebec's Christmas season.

tlers in the province of Quebec. Although it is popular throughout Canada, it is most associated with réveillons (REV-ay-yohns), traditional French-Canadian Christmas Eve gatherings. Food blogger Sarah Louise, who grew up in Quebec, recalls the réveillons of her childhood:

> My mother … and her four sisters would attend church for midnight mass …while back at home, Memère (my maternal grandmother) would busy herself cooking. … When the crowd would return home with other family members and friends in tow, a buffet of

Tourtière

Tourtière is made with ground meat. Pork or beef can be used. This recipe uses beef.

Ingredients
2 9-inch pie shells (for the top and bottom)
1 ½ lbs. ground beef
1 ½ cups mashed potatoes
¼ cup chopped onions
¼ teaspoon each of nutmeg, allspice, cinnamon, salt, pepper
½ cup water

Directions
1. Cook the meat, spices, and onions in the water over medium heat until the meat is no longer pink, about 30 minutes, stirring often.
2. Preheat the oven to 450°F. Remove the cooked meat from the stove. Stir the mashed potatoes into the meat mixture. Let the mixture cool for five minutes.
3. Line a pie pan with a pie shell. Spoon in the meat mixture. Cover with the other pie shell. Cut an X in the top of the crust. Bake until the crust is browned, about 30 minutes.

Makes one pie. Serves 6–8.

rich comfort food would be readily available to welcome in the cold and weary travelers. . . . The tourtière is the single most common dish consumed by the Quebecois [residents of Quebec] at Christmas."[14]

There are many ways to make a tourtière. The pie

can vary in size from small to large and enough to serve eighteen people. Ingredients also vary. Traditionally, a tourtière is filled with ground pork spiced with cinnamon, allspice, nutmeg, and cloves. In the past, the spices were added to preserve the pork. Modern cooks prize the spices for the earthy flavor and scent they give the dish.

The filling is cooked before it is totally surrounded by pie crust. Then the pie is baked until the crust is golden. According to Stewart, "As it browns and bubbles it perfumes the entire house."[15] And, when it is finally served it tastes amazing.

Christmas Pastries

Most Canadians have another big meal on Christmas Day. Menus vary, but special cakes and cookies are almost always eaten. Dropping in to see friends and family throughout the holiday season is a popular practice in Canada. Friendly Canadians bake pastries such as shortbread and gingerbread cookies before Christmas to serve to unexpected guests. Scottish settlers first brought the practice of serving shortbread at Christmastime to Canada. Shortbread cookies are sweet butter cookies that originated in Scotland. Dark spicy gingerbread cookies, flavored with sugar, ginger, and molasses, were brought to Canada by German settlers. Canadian homesteaders formed gingerbread dough into the shape of children. They then baked the dough, decorated the baked cookies with icing, and hung them on the Christmas tree.

Dogsledding

Dogsleds are small sleds pulled by dogs on which the rider usually stands. Packs of dogs that have been bred over centuries to withstand the cold are trained to work together pulling the sled. Dog teams can travel up to 80 miles (130km) a day at speeds up to 20 miles per hour (30kph).

Dog sledding holds an important place in Canadian history. In the past the Inuit, or native people of Canada's far north, depended on dog sleds for transportation. Dogsleds were used to deliver mail and supplies to northern communities, and the Canadian Mounted Police used them to patrol areas where horses were impractical.

The invention of the snowmobile largely replaced the need for dogsleds. However, dogsled racing has become a popular sport in Canada. The longest dog race held in Canada, the YukonQuest, covers 960 miles (1,600 km).

A special pastry, called Bûche de Noël (boosh duh no-EL), or Yule log, is reserved for Christmas dinner. Bûche de Noël is a French-Canadian specialty that came to Canada from France. The cake is both delicious and a work of art. It is a light sponge cake that is filled with rich, sweet buttercream, then rolled up to look like a log. Chocolate frosting is spread over the outside and made to look like bark. The ends of the log are coated with vanilla cream to resemble freshly cut wood. Pieces of chocolate-covered cake are added to the log to represent little twigs and branches. The whole creation is decorated with fresh berries, leaves

The Bûche de Noël is beautifully decorated to look like a log, complete with bark, twigs, and leaves.

made from green frosting, tiny mushrooms made of meringue (muh-RANG) (a mixture of stiff beaten egg whites and sugar), and powdered sugar to resemble snow. "It's so lovely it's a shame to eat it,"[16] says Barss. Of course, it is also too delicious to resist.

Delicious and special foods like Bûche de Noël add to the joy and fun of Canadian celebrations. They help make the festivities more memorable.

Metric Conversions

Mass (weight)

1 ounce (oz.)	= 28.0 grams (g)
8 ounces	= 227.0 grams
1 pound (lb.) or 16 ounces	= 0.45 kilograms (kg)
2.2 pounds	= 1.0 kilogram

Liquid Volume

1 teaspoon (tsp.)	= 5.0 milliliters (ml)
1 tablespoon (tbsp.)	= 15.0 milliliters
1 fluid ounce (oz.)	= 30.0 milliliters
1 cup (c.)	= 240 milliliters
1 pint (pt.)	= 480 milliliters
1 quart (qt.)	= 0.96 liters (l)
1 gallon (gal.)	= 3.84 liters

Pan Sizes

8-inch cake pan	= 20 x 4-centimeter cake pan
9-inch cake pan	= 23 x 3.5-centimeter cake pan
11 x 7-inch baking pan	= 28 x 18-centimeter baking pan
13 x 9-inch baking pan	= 32.5 x 23-centimeter baking pan
9 x 5-inch loaf pan	= 23 x 13-centimeter loaf pan
2-quart casserole	= 2-liter casserole

Temperature

212°F	= 100°C (boiling point of water)
225°F	= 110°C
250°F	= 120°C
275°F	= 135°C
300°F	= 150°C
325°F	= 160°C
350°F	= 180°C
375°F	= 190°C
400°F	= 200°C

Length

1/4 inch (in.)	= 0.6 centimeters (cm)
1/2 inch	= 1.25 centimeters
1 inch	= 2.5 centimeters

Notes

Chapter 1: Land of Plenty

1. Quoted in "The Return." Inuit Gallery of Vancouver. www.inuit.com/page236.htm.
2. Quoted in Dorothy Duncan. *Canadians at Table.* Toronto: Dundurn, 2006, p. 27.
3. Anita Stewart. *The Flavours of Canada.* Vancouver, BC: Raincoast, 2000, p. 71.
4. Ryan Skelton. "Sugar Shacks and a Sweet Tooth." Countertop Buzz, March 23, 2009. http://countertopbuzz.ca/sugar-shacks-and-sweet-tooth.

Chapter 2: A Diverse Nation

5. Ryan Skelton. "Nova Scotia Seafood Chowder." Countertop Buzz, January 30, 2009. http://countertopbuzz.ca/nova-scotia-seafood-chowder.
6. Bunny Barss. *Oh, Canada!* Regina, Saskatchewan: Centax of Canada, 1987, p. 162.
7. David Katz. "Taste Canada My Flavors of Canada—A Blog in Honor of Canada Day." Kitchen Savvy, June 27, 2005. http://kitchensavvy.typepad.com/journal/2005/06/taste_canada_wh.html#ixzz1HHGud3QD.

Chapter 3: Uniquely Canadian Treats

8. A. Knight. "Poutine 101." Knight's Canadian Info Collection. http://members.shaw.ca/kcic1/poutine.html.

9. Jessie Oleson. "You Say Nanaimo: Words, Praise, and Lore on the Heavenly Nanaimo Bar." Cake Spy.com, May 26, 2008. www.cakespy.com/blog-old/2008/5/27/you-say-nanaimo-words-praise-and-lore-on-the-heavenly-nanaim.html.

10. Lynette Stanley-Maddocks. "Bannock and Wild Blueberry Jam." Lex Culinaria, June 27, 2005. http://gorgeoustown.typepad.com/lex_culinaria/2005/06/bannock_and_blu.html.

11. Stanley-Maddocks. "Bannock and Wild Blueberry Jam."

Chapter 4: Festive Food

12. Stewart. *The Flavours of Canada*, p. 66.

13. Quoted in "What Makes a Good Butter Tart?" The CBC Digital Archives Website, Canadian Broadcasting Corporation, December 5, 1991. Last Updated June 29, 2004. http://archives.cbc.ca/lifestyle/food/clips/8373.

14. Sarah Louise. "Christmas in Quebec Updated Conclusion." One Whole Clove, December 23, 2005. http://onewholeclove.typepad.com/one_whole_clove/2005/12/christmas_in_qu_5.html.

15. Stewart. *The Flavours of Canada*, p. 155.

16. Barss. *Oh, Canada!*, p. 115.

Glossary

bannock: A flat, round type of fried bread.

bison: A large, shaggy animal also known as a buffalo.

butter tarts: Little pastries filled with a mixture of butter, sugar, eggs, raisins, and maple syrup.

chuck wagon: A wagon that carried food and cooking tools to serve people working outdoors, like cowboys.

clambake: An event in which clams and/or other seafood is cooked in a pit lined with hot stones and seaweed.

First Nations: The name given collectively to the various tribes of Canada's native people.

Grand Banks: A rich fishing area located off the coast of Newfoundland.

marinate: To soak food in a liquid in order to flavor the food.

pemmican: A staple food of the First Nations of the prairies consisting of dried meat mixed with berries and animal fat.

poutine: A Canadian fast food made up of fried potatoes topped with cheese curds and gravy.

province: A division of a country similar to a state.

sugar shacks: Makeshift buildings where maple sap is boiled in large vats until syrup forms.

tourtière: A Canadian meat pie that originated in France.

wild rice: A nutty-tasting grain that grows on a type of wild grass.

For Further Exploration

Books

Vivien Bower. *Wow Canada! Exploring This Land from Coast to Coast.* Toronto, ON: Maple Tree, 2009. This book takes readers on a trip through Canada with great illustrations, maps, and information on climate, geography, and wildlife.

Carlotta Hacker. *The Kids Book of Canadian History.* Toronto, ON: Kids Can., 2009. This nicely illustrated book looks at Canada's history.

Bobbie Kalman. *Canada: The Culture.* New York: Crabtree, 2009. The focus is on Canadian myths, holidays, and culture with photos and illustrations.

Bobbie Kalman. *Canada: The Land.* New York: Crabtree, 2009. This book looks at Canada's geography, climate, and landforms with maps and photos.

Websites

Canadian Geographic "Canadian Geographic Kids!" (www.canadiangeographic.ca/kids/). This offers lots of information and pictures about Canada, Canadian wildlife, fun facts, games, and maps just for kids.

Food by Country "Canada" (www.foodbycountry. com/Algeria-to-France/Canada.html). Gives information about Canadian geography, history, government, holidays, and food with recipes.

Library and Archives Canada "The Learning Centre" (www.collectionscanada.gc.ca/education/008-2011-e. html). This website provides links to all kinds of information on Canada including geography, history, natural resources, the First Nations, hockey, the flag, a virtual museum, and Canadian statistics.

National Geographic Kids "Canada" (http://kids. nationalgeographic.com/kids/places/find/canada/). Facts about Canada's geography, history, culture, and wildlife with colored photos, a video, maps, and an e-postcard.

Index

Picture Credits

About the Author

Barbara Sheen is the author of more than 60 books for young people. She lives in New Mexico with her family. In her spare time, she likes to swim, walk, garden, and read. Of course, she loves to cook!